TOP TEN LONGEST WONDERS ON EARTH

BY JOHN ALLAN

CONTENTS

WELCOME TO THE WORLD'S LONGEST!	4
LONGEST PASSENGER TRAIN	6
LONGEST MONSTER TRUCK JUMP	8
LONGEST RIVER	10
LONGEST REPTILE	12
LONGEST CONTAINER SHIP	14
LONGEST BEETLE	16
LONGEST INSECT	18
LONGEST ZIP WIRE	20
LONGEST STRUCTURE	22
LONGEST-NECKED ANIMAL	24
LONGEST LIFESPANS	26
CLOSE, BUT NOT CLOSE ENOUGH!	28
THE PEOPLE BEHIND THE RECORDS	30
GLOSSARY	31
INDEX	32

Copyright © 2025 Hungry Tomato Ltd

First published in 2025 by Hungry Tomato Ltd
F15, Old Bakery Studios, Blewetts Wharf, Malpas Road, Truro, Cornwall, TR1 1QH, UK.

No part of this publication may be reproduced, stored in a retrieval system, or transmitted in any form or by any means, electronic, mechanical, photocopying, recording, or otherwise, without prior written permission of the copyright owner.

A CIP catalogue record for this book is available from the British Library.

ISBN 9781835694220

Printed in China

Discover more at
www.hungrytomato.com

Words in **BOLD** can be found in the glossary.

WELCOME TO THE WORLD'S LONGEST!

We live on a planet with so many impressive things. Prepare to be amazed by some of the world's longest record-breakers…

MADE BY HUMANS AND NATURE

The longest things in the world come in all shapes and sizes. Some are incredible wonders of nature, from landscapes to animals, and others are incredible human-made things.

MEASURING SIZE

You can usually see when something is long, but how can you tell exactly how long it is? Length is measured from one end of something to the other end. The longest things in the world are usually written as miles, or kilometres (km).

MAKING HISTORY

We have found so many incredible record-breaking things on our planet, but there are still so many places we haven't explored yet. Modern technology is getting better all the time, so new things are being uncovered all the time by people whose names will go down in history!

HOLDING ONTO A RECORD

Humans are always hoping their creations will break records. People across the world are always competing to build bigger, longer, and even more impressive structures to achieve these dreams. This means that records are constantly changing.

This book showcases 10 of the longest things in the world!
It's hard to compare these record-breakers as they are all so different. What's long for an animal may seem short compared to some forms of transport, but it's still impressive. The top 10 in this book are in no particular order, but everyone will have a favourite!

1 LONGEST PASSENGER TRAIN

The longest passenger train in the world (with regular services) is The Ghan. Found in Australia, this train runs from Darwin to Adelaide, through the outback, which is also one of the longest rail rides on the continent.

Like most trains, carriages can be added and removed from The Ghan, depending on how many people are on board. At its longest, this mighty piece of machinery pulls 44 carriages, making it more than half a mile (1 km) long!

This impressively long train has been operating for almost 100 years and it's estimated that more than 40,000 people travel on it every year.

DID YOU KNOW?

The Ghan is long, but it's not the longest train ever. That record goes to a BHP Iron Ore freight train built to transport **mined** material. It was 4.5 miles (7.2 km) long!

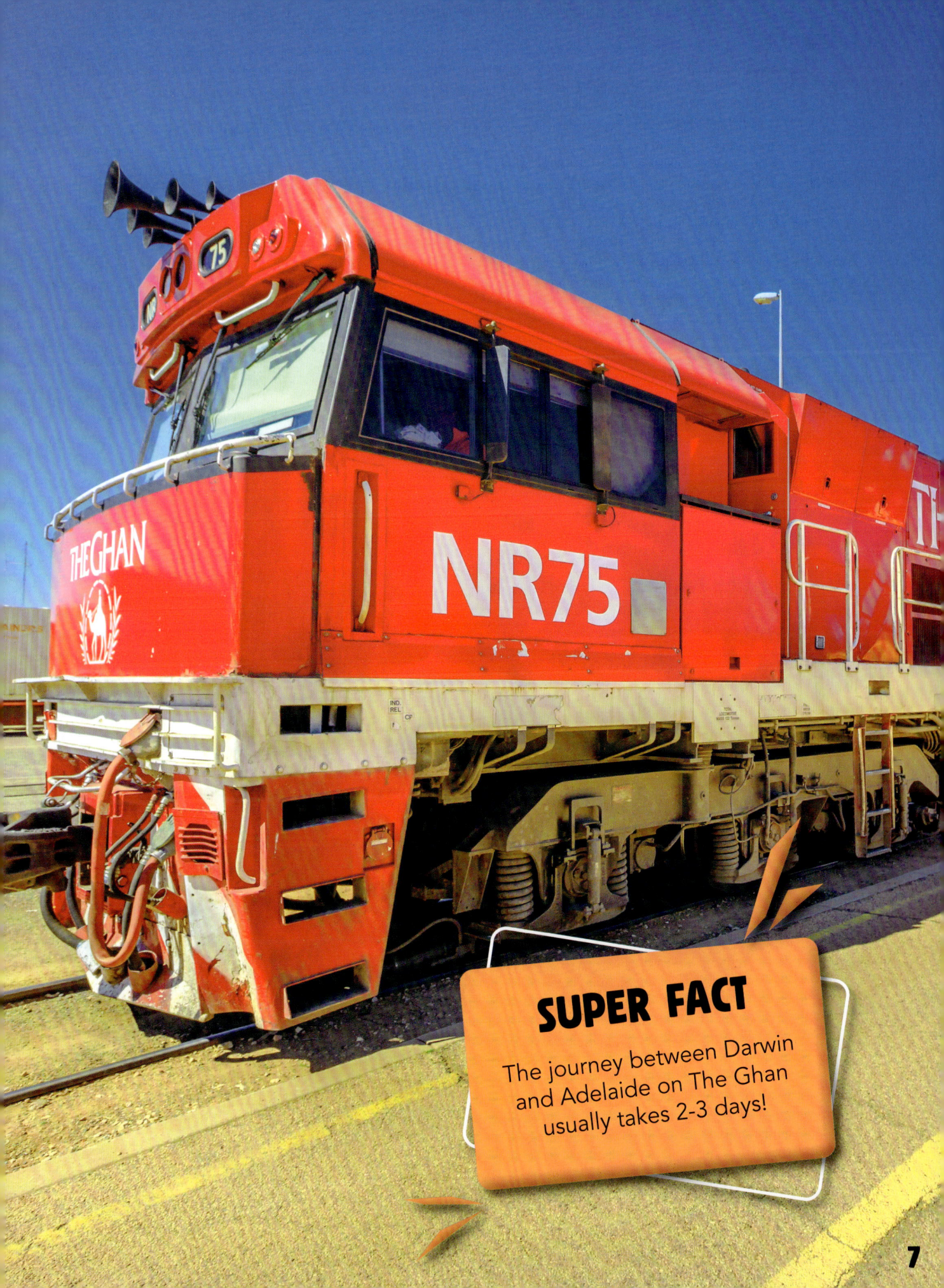

SUPER FACT

The journey between Darwin and Adelaide on The Ghan usually takes 2-3 days!

2 LONGEST MONSTER TRUCK JUMP

The record for longest monster truck jump has been held for more than 10 years by "Bad Habit".

In 2013, the truck charged up a ramp and jumped over 72 metres (237 ft) through the air. Bad Habit had been modified by owner, Joe Sylvester, who used it to compete in lots of monster truck events.

What makes the record more impressive is that the truck weighs 4,535 kilograms (10,000 lbs) — the same as two adult rhinos!

SUPER FACT

Joe Sylvester also holds the world record for the fastest speed achieved by a monster truck. He hit 101.8 miles per hour (163.8 km/h).

DID YOU KNOW?

Monster trucks can jump high and far because they have incredibly powerful engines and massive wheels to help with takeoff, as well as strong **shock absorbers** which help with landing.

3 LONGEST RIVER

The world's longest river is the Nile, which runs through 11 countries in northeastern Africa before reaching the Mediterranean Sea.

DID YOU KNOW?

To keep the river flowing steadily, a dam has been built along the Nile in Aswan, Egypt. As well as controlling how much water is flowing, it uses the water's power to **generate** electricity.

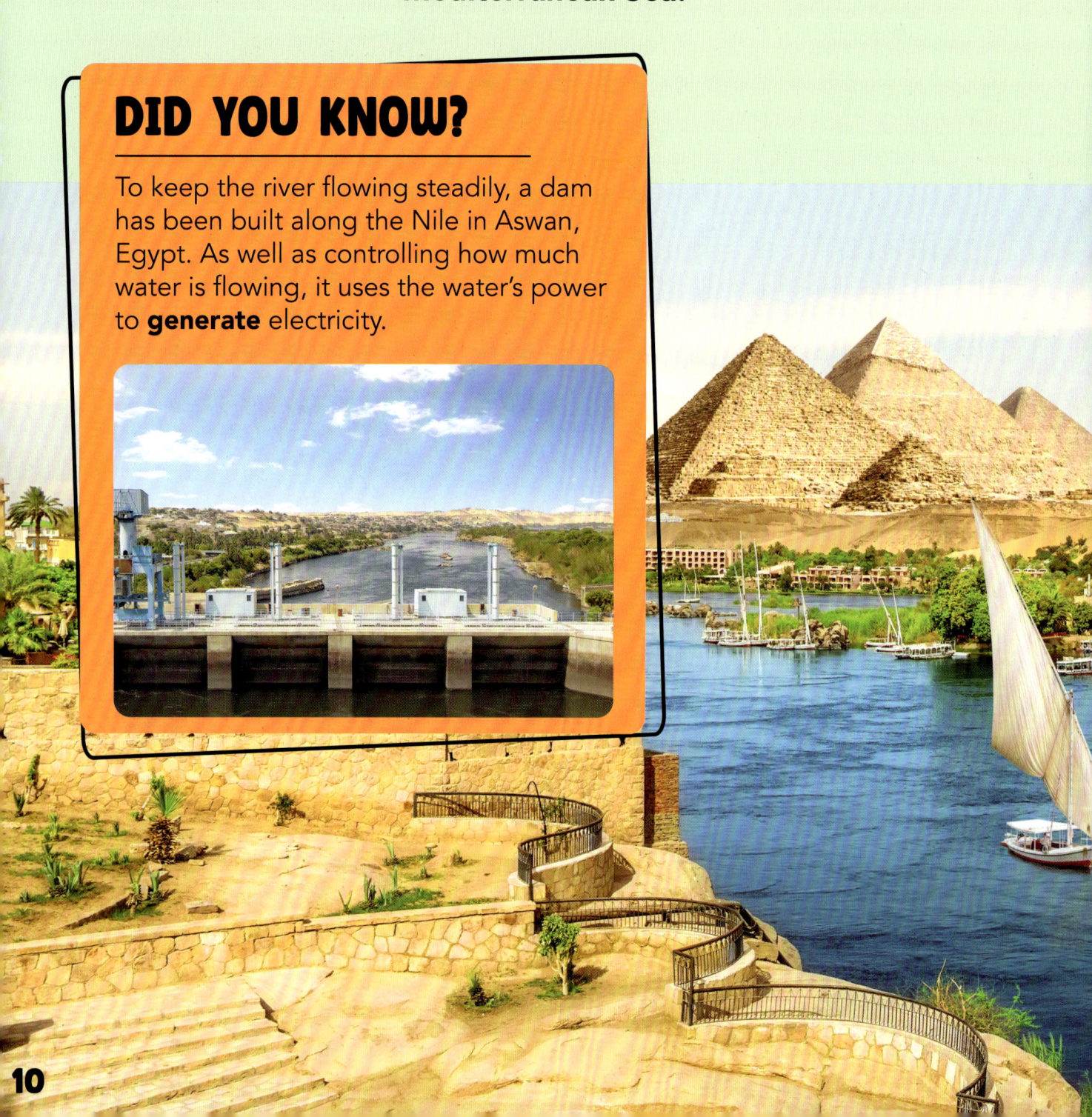

The Nile River travels more than 4,200 miles (6,700 km) in total, and has provided nearby areas with water for washing, drinking, growing crops, and transporting goods for thousands of years.

Although the Nile has been considered the longest river for years, some people argue that the Amazon river is longer. It depends on what you consider to be the start and end of a river.

SUPER FACT

It's not safe to swim in the Nile because it's home to the ferocious Nile crocodile!

4 LONGEST REPTILE

The reticulated python is the longest reptile in the world. The top length ever recorded was 10 metres (33 ft) – that's almost as long as a school bus!

These snakes are clever hunters, and not afraid to **prey** on big animals like wild boar, deer, and monkeys. There have even been rare occasions of them eating people!

Despite their size, reticulated pythons can strike prey with lightning speed, grabbing them with their teeth and wrapping their long body around to cut off air supply. Like many snakes, they have incredibly stretchy skin around their jaws which allow them to swallow even the biggest prey whole!

DID YOU KNOW?

The patterns of the reticulated python's scales provide perfect **camouflage** in its **tropical rainforest** home, helping it stay out of the sight of prey until it's ready to attack!

SUPER FACT

Reticulated pythons are the longest living snakes in the world, and are in the top three of heaviest snakes too.

5 LONGEST CONTAINER SHIP

The world record for longest container ship is shared between several vehicles that have all measured 400 metres (1,300 ft). This includes Tihama, Mol Triumph, and Baltic Breeze.

The record-breaking ships come from different countries and travel around the world, transporting goods and products.

The Tihana (pictured) usually carries about 20,000 containers. Impressively, container ships that are only 2 cm (4 inches) shorter than the Tihana have broken a record by carrying 24,000 containers!

SUPER FACT

For land vehicles, we measure speed in miles (or km) per hour, but for ships, we measure in knots. Knots allow for wind speed and the curve of the Earth. Cargo ships normally move at around 20-25 knots.

DID YOU KNOW?

Container ships may never get any bigger or be able to beat this record. If they were bigger, they would struggle to fit in **ports**, turn in **canals**, and be more at risk of tipping over during storms.

6 LONGEST BEETLE

Deep in the tropical rainforests of Central and South America lives the world's longest beetle, the Hercules beetle!

The Hercules beetle is a type of rhinoceros beetle, a group named after the long horns that grow on their heads. It's because of their horns that Hercules beetles are called the longest in the world – all in all, the males can grow up to 19 cm (7.5 inches) long!

SUPER FACT
If you only measure body length, the titan beetle is the longest. Its body can be almost 17 cm (6.6 inches). Without their horns, Hercules beetles only measure 8.5 cm (3.5 inches).

Hercules beetles horns don't just look impressive – they're useful. The horns are mostly used to fight off other males during **mating season**, similar to how deer use their antlers to fight.

DID YOU KNOW?

Hercules beetles are named after the **mythological** ancient Greek hero, Hercules, who was said to be an incredibly strong fighter.

7 LONGEST INSECT

Beetles may be lengthy, but they're not the longest insect in the world! That award goes to a stick insect.

The longest stick insect ever recorded belongs to a group without an official name! It's informally called *Phryganistria chinensis*. It was found in China, and measured an incredible 64 cm (2 ft) with its legs fully outstretched.

This record-breaker was announced in 2017 when it dethroned the previous record-holder, and there's an unbelievable connection. The previous record-holder was a stick insect belonging to the same group and it was the grandmother of the new record-breaker!

DID YOU KNOW?

Stick insects blend into their surroundings, making them hard to spot. This camouflage protects them from **predators**.

SUPER FACT

If a predator attacks and pulls a stick insect's leg off, the stick insect may still be able to escape. They don't have to worry about the missing leg – they can grow it back!

8 LONGEST ZIP WIRE

The Jais Flight in the UAE holds the record for being the longest single span of zip wire in the world!

This daring zip wire is an incredible 1.76 miles (2.8 km) long. It launches from the Jebel Jais mountain top that's 1 mile (1.7 km) above sea level.

Daring adventurers who take a flight on the zip wire get to soar through mountains and over ravines at speeds of up to 93 miles per hour (150 km/h)! It only takes 3 minutes to reach the bottom when moving that quickly.

DID YOU KNOW?

Since its opening in 2018, over 70,000 people have experienced the Jebel Jais zip wire.

SUPER FACT

The Jais Flight zip wire is located in the Hajar mountains. Scientists who have studied the mountains' rocks found that millions of years ago they were deep under the sea!

9 LONGEST STRUCTURE

The Great Wall of China is the longest human-made structure in the world. It was built to defend the Chinese Empire from its enemies.

The wall runs over mountains and plains, with towers dotted along the wall to help with defence. It stretches from the Gobi desert in the west to the Beijing coast on the east, covering a total of 12,500 miles (20,000 km). That's double the length of England!

The Great Wall took more than 2,000 years to construct, with many generations building and rebuilding different sections. Because of this, some sections are made of different materials, like stone, wood, or mud.

DID YOU KNOW?

More than 10 million people visit the Great Wall of China every year!

SUPER FACT

Scientists have found that parts of the wall were stuck together with sticky rice flour! It must be strong – it's survived for centuries.

10 LONGEST-NECKED ANIMAL

The longest-necked animal that ever existed was the Mamenchisaurus, a plant-eating dinosaur that lived 160 million years ago!

This record-breaking dinosaur's neck was estimated to be almost 15 metres (50 ft) long! That's eight times the length of a giraffe's neck, which are the longest necks of animals living today.

Scientists discovered **fossils** of this dinosaur for the first time in 1987, but they didn't have many to study. More recent fossil finds have led to them truly understanding the size of this **prehistoric** neck!

DID YOU KNOW?

Mamenchisaurus belonged to a group of dinosaurs called sauropods. They all had long necks. Scientists think their necks grew so long to help them reach food from incredibly tall trees.

SUPER FACT

Mamenchisaurus may have the longest neck, but it's thought that it had a small body and short tail by comparison.

LONGEST LIFESPANS

Some things aren't long to look at – they are long in terms of time! Here are some of the longest living things ever.

LONGEST-LIVED PERSON

Frenchwoman Jeanne Calment was born in 1875 and died in 1997. That's the longest recorded **lifespan** of any human – 122 years and 164 days. Jeanne proved that age doesn't have to be a barrier. She was very active, and rode a bicycle until the age of 100!

METHUSELAH

LONGEST-LIVED TREE

The oldest recorded tree ever was a bristlecone pine called Prometheus. It was thought to be about 5,200 years old when it was cut down. The oldest tree living today is also a bristlecone pine. Methuselah is 4,857 in 2025, meaning it's got a while until it overtakes Prometheus!

LONGEST-LIVED ANIMAL

A Seychelles giant tortoise named Jonathan holds the world record for being the longest-living land animal ever known. He is thought to have been born in 1832, making him 193 in 2025.

CLOSE, BUT NOT CLOSE ENOUGH!

There are lots of amazingly long things on Earth that didn't quite make our top ten. Here are some impressive runners-up.

LONGEST LEGS

Ostriches have the longest legs of any living bird. They can cover 3 to 5 metres (10–16 ft) in just one step, which also makes them the fastest-running birds in the world.

LONGEST PLACE NAME

The longest place name in the world is the 168-letter official name for Bangkok, the capital of Thailand: *krung thep mahanakhon amon rattanakosin mahinthara ayuthaya mahadilok phop noppharat ratchathani burirom udomratchaniwet mahasathan amon piman awatan sathit sakkathattiya witsanukam prasit.*

LONGEST MAMMAL MIGRATION

Lots of animals **migrate** every year, but humpback whales have one of the longest journeys. They have the longest **mammal** migration, journeying 5,100 miles (8,200 km) each way between the equator and the polar regions.

LONGEST HORNS

The animal with the longest horns ever is the Asian water buffalo. The average length is 1 metre (3 ft), but some individuals have been recorded with horns almost 4 metres (14 ft) from tip to tip!

LONGEST CLAWS

The longest animal claws ever known are the fossil claws of therizinosauridae – a group of dinosaurs that lived about 70 million years ago. They measured up to 90 cm (3 ft) long!

THE PEOPLE BEHIND THE RECORDS

Humans have discovered and created some incredible things throughout history. Here's just some of the people behind the amazing records in this book.

JOHANN SCHNEIDER & FRANÇOIS DAUDIN

Johann Schneider was the first person to write a scientific description of the reticulated python, but he gave it a different name – he called it "Boa reticulata". The name "Python" was suggested by François Daudin in 1803.

QIN SHI HUANG

Around 220 BCE, the First Emperor of China, Qui Shi Huang, decided that all the defensive walls in the country should be joined together. This was the beginning of the Great Wall of China.

JOHN MCDOUALL STUART

The route that The Ghan, the world's longest train, follows is based on the route that John McDouall Stuart took when exploring Australia in the 1800s.

GLOSSARY

Camouflage – the way animals blend in with their surroundings so they can't be seen easily.

Canals – narrow waterways that were made by humans to connect two bodies of water.

Continent – one of the huge pieces of land on Earth. For example, Africa and North America are separate continents.

Fossils – the remains or impression of plants and animals that lived long ago.

Generate – to make.

Lifespan – the length of time a human or animal lives.

Mammal – a type of warm-blooded animal (including humans) that produce milk to feed their young.

Mating season – the time of year when animals mate to produce babies.

Migrate – when animals move from one place to another, usually to find food or because of changes in the weather.

Mined - dug up from underground.

Mythological – something which is based on a made-up story, but that at one time people believed in.

Ports – sheltered places where ships stop to load or unload cargo.

Predators – animals that hunt other animals for food.

Prehistoric – the time before humans existed.

Prey – to hunt other animals.

Shock absorbers – part of the suspension of a vehicle that helps it move smoothly.

Tropical rainforest – a forest that is very hot and wet, and the plants grow closely together.

31

INDEX

A
Amazon river 11
Asian water buffalo 29

B
Bad Habit (monster truck) 8-9
Baltic Breeze (container ship) 14
Bangkok, Thailand 28
BHP Iron Ore (train) 6
Bristlecone pine 27

C
Calment, Jeanne 26

D
Daudin, François 30

G
Great Wall of China 22-23, 30

H
Hercules beetles 16-17
Hercules (Greek hero) 17
Huang, Qin Shi 30
Humpback whale 29

J
Jais Fight Zip Wire, Jebel Jais, UAE 20-21

M
Mamenchisaurus 24-25
Methuselah (tree) 27
Mol Triumph (container ship) 14

N
Nile river, Africa 10-11

O
Ostrich 28

P
Phryganistria chinensis stick insect 18-19
Prometheus (tree) 27

R
Reticulated python 12-13, 30

S
Schneider, Johann 30
Seychelles giant tortoise 27
Stuart, John McDouall 30
Sylvester, Joe 8

T
Therizinosauridae 29
The Ghan, Australia (train) 6-7, 30
Tihama (container ship) 14-15
Titan beetle 16

Picture credits:
Abbreviations: m-middle, t-top, l-left, r-right, bg-background.

Wikipedia: By Unknown author - http://collections.slsa.sa.gov.au/resource/B+501., Public Domain, https://commons.wikimedia.org/w/index.php?curid=82490250 30bl; By Joachim Bresseel and Jérôme Constant - Giant sticks from Vietnam and China, with three new taxa including the second longest insect known to date (Phasmatodea, Phasmatidae, Clitumninae, Pharnaciini)". European Journal of Taxonomy 104: 1–38 (2014). https://dx.doi.org/10.5852/ejt.2014.104, CC BY-SA 3.0, https://commons.wikimedia.org/w/index.php?curid=45011060 5tl, 18-19bg; By Yuya Tamai from Gifu, Japan - 2014-03-25 12.46.44, CC BY 2.0, https://commons.wikimedia.org/w/index.php?curid=31836654 29bl. Shutterstock: 27tl; Adwo 6b; agsaz 10bl; Alex Anton 10-11bg; Benny Marty 7bg; divi putra stock 12br; feathercollector 4tl, 17-18bg; Green Oak 15br; jaimantaip 13bg; 30ml; Javen 22br; Kostiantyn Ivanyshen 24-25bg, 24bm; Ligankov Aleksey 17mr; luckyluke007 3b, 9tr; Lysenji Andrii 4br; Mark Brandon 19tr; MartinLueke 14-15bg; Oleksandr Chernysh 20b; shutter_o 28br; sirisak_baokaew 29mr; Snapper Nick 27br; Snaptheframe 21bg, 31b; Subphoto.com 29tl; Tavarius 28ml; Yuri Yavnik 5, 23bg, 30mr.

Every effort has been made to trace the copyright holders, and we apologise in advance for any unintentional omissions. We would be pleased to insert the appropriate acknowledgements in any subsequent edition of this publication.